RELAXATION TIPS FOR YOUR SOUL

OVERCOMING ANXIETY

WRITTEN BY
GLENDA COKER

TERMS AND CONDITIONS

Notice: -The author of this information used the best efforts in preparing this material. The content contained here is for learning purposes. God bless you.

DISCLAIMER

All content including cover design is not to be copied, reproduced, sold, distributed, modified, deviated, transmitted, displayed anywhere including networks, blogs or websites. Any use of this content and or cover design is strictly prohibited. –2016, ISBN 978-1-7356677-7-5

TABLE OF CONTENTS

Chapter 1: Uncontrolled Anxiety Introduction

Chapter 2: Managing Uncontrolled Anxiety

Chapter 3: Stay Focused

Chapter 4: Distractions

Chapter 5: Muscle Relaxation to Control Anxiety

Chapter 6: Anxiety from Interviews, Test Taking and Meetings

7. Conclusion

8. Opportunity

9. Bible Scriptures

10. About the Author

FOREWORD

Anxiety itself is not terrible. Trouble arises when anxiety escalates and is hard to control. If you are often stressed and out of control without a reason, you are a victim of escalated anxiety. Each anxiety situation causes personality shifts.

We face many complications in life. You may become tired and frustrated to the point of anger. These emotions can be controlled. Effective measures are needed to control anxieties.

Anxiety is an act emotion. In emergency situations, feelings of anxiety are escalated. If you do not let your emotions get out of control, your move to safety is quicker. Too often, anxiety is overexerted. The reasons anxiety gets out of control depends on the source. It may be trauma, emotional or a phobia. Once the cause is identified, you can begin to heal.

It might sound strange, but controlled anxiety along with anger and similar emotions can protect and move you away from harm. If used in the proper perspectives, these emotions can save your life. In these pages, I cover obsessive anxiety behaviors and management control techniques.

CHAPTER 1:

UNCONTROLLED ANXIETY INTRODUCTION

In this chapter, you will be introduced to the concepts of anxiety. In addition, you will learn:

v TYPES OF

ANXIETY

v TREATMENTS

HOW IS ANXIETY GOOD?

Life is full of tension, stress and problems. Everyone handles intensities in their own ways. Anxiety can be positive or negative depending on how you control it.

You may wonder how anxiety can be positive. Take for instance, you see an elderly person crossing the street on a red light and cars are coming. You are frightened. You wave cars to slow them down and run to assist the person to safety.

The anxiety within you moved the person out of danger. If you had no anxiety to do this, the person may have lost their life. In this example, anxiety is controlled and effective. At times, we overexert ourselves and that is when we face problems.

SIT BACK AND RELAX

Sit back and relax.

You deserve some slack.

Enjoy a day at the beach, playing in the sand with your earphones on listening to your favorite band.

OR

Simply enjoy a full day at the park, not leaving until after dark.

HOW IS ANXIETY BEHAVIOR BAD?

TO STRUGGLE:

Make forceful or violent efforts to get free of restraint or constriction.

Example: If you struggle to focus and gain control, anxiety increases. For example, some students are nervous and anxious when it comes to test taking. This leads to mistakes and erases memory. The student does poor on the exam and may fail.

PANIC ATTACK:

A sudden episode of intense fear, triggering physical reactions when there is no apparent cause or real danger.

A panic attack can be very frightening. One might think they are having a heart attack, losing control of emotions, or even dying.

If anxiety is out of control, it can get severe enough to escalate into a panic attack. A panic attack is a severe disorder. You become nervous and upset. Your heart is racing, and blood pressure is increasing. You may be dizzy as if to faint. This disorder is intense and escalates beyond the stages of an anxiety disorder.

Anxiety weights down the heart, but a kind word cheers it up.

Proverbs 12: 25 [4]

PHOBIA

A phobia occurs when you hold fear and worry in your mind. For instance, you may be scared of heights. You worry each time you go upstairs at home or use an elevator at work. This is a phobia and life events trigger these emotions.

I sought the LORD, and He answered me and delivered me from all my fears.

Psalm 34:4 [16]

A DISORDER IS:

A condition that affects your behavior, feelings, mood and thinking.

TREATMENT OF DISORDERS

Often, people believe that panic attacks, phobias, anxiety and the similar is treated and cured with medicine. Medicine holds the role of a temporary mask. Mind therapy is the second best long term reliever. God is number one over all things. Put your courage, faith, trust and belief in HIM who will see you through any circumstance. May all your glory be to God.

"Glory to God in the highest, and on earth peace, good will towards men!"

Luke 2:14

CHAPTER 2:

MANAGING UNCONTROLLED ANXIETY

This chapter brings you to a deeper level of anxiety management.

YOU WILL LEARN HOW TO:

- **CATEGORIZE ANXIETY FROM 1-10**

- **CAREFULLY MONITOR ANXIETY LEVELS**

- **REMAIN PRESENT**

- **TAKE ON FEARS**

- **STAY CALM**

- FIGURE OUT BAD THOUGHTS

- TAKE CONTROL OF YOUR THOUGHTS AND FEELINGS

- LOCATE THE TRIGGER POINTS OF ANXIETY

- STAY WITHIN YOURSELF

- TAKE CONTROL OF ANXIETY DISORDERS

- TAKE CARE OF EMOTIONS

Therapies for anxiety and similar disorders are in the hundreds. They promise solutions but most take an excess of time and are hard to follow. There may be times when anxiety management skills are tested most when you least expect it.

You may not know how to stay calm, which leads you to overreact. We are born into an imperfect life and at times emotions are harder to control. To have control, you need to be ready to expect the unexpected. Ask God for guidance through prayer and supplication.

May my supplication come before you; deliver me according to your promise.

Psalm 119:170

STAY CALM

CATEGORIZE ANXIETY LEVELS FROM 1-10

Be sure to monitor your anxiety levels. Self-measurement can be tricky, but with practice, you will be fine. Pay attention to the things that give you the most anxiety. Write them down and categorize them from 1 to 10, with 10 being the highest.

CAREFULLY MONITOR YOUR ACTIVITY LEVELS

Once the levels of anxiety are written, watch your mood swings. Which emotions are you experiencing and at what times of the day? What mood are you in? You will find the more you worry, anxiety levels increase. When you stop worrying as much, you forget the problem exists. Accept what is happening to you in these moments. Stay calm and do not become upset. The anxious moment is temporary and will pass through with prayer and supplication.

Jesus looked at them and said, "With man this is impossible, but not with God; all things are possible with God".

Mark 10:27

THE PRESENT

Another important technique is to say the *what is* rather than *what if*. Do not concern yourself with the future. You hold zero control on what happens. Your concentration needs to be on the present. Make your present life happier and the future will be better. No worries on what comes in the future when your present life needs attention. God is with you! Live your life in peace.

READ, REST, PRAY AND RELAX

Therefore do not worry about tomorrow, for tomorrow will worry about itself. Each day has enough trouble of its own.

Matthew 6:34

DO NOT ESCAPE FROM YOURSELF

Out of fear, people may run from troubles. This is not a good idea. If you escape, it may take you away from the problem, but it will not solve it. The problem continues no matter where you go. It is best to take action at that moment before moving on. The consequences may be greater if you try to push away without a solution. A fear technique you will learn is how to face fears with courage. Ask yourself:

What is bothering you? Why are you afraid? Do you want to run? Erase wanting to escape. Have faith in God that HE will pull you through!

The LORD is my light and my salvation; whom shall I fear? The LORD is the stronghold of my life; of whom shall I be afraid?

Psalm 27:1

Fear of man will prove to be a snare, but whoever trusts in the LORD is kept safe.

Proverbs 29:25

SOOTHE YOUR MIND IN HIGH ANXIETY LEVELS

Realize your limits. Do not accelerate anxiety. Once you do, you get upset with yourself. You will lose your positive thoughts, blocking you from rational thinking. At times, you may struggle and that is okay. Do not lose confidence. Have faith you will over-power any problems through prayer and the grace of the Almighty God.

Now faith is confidence in what we hope for and assurance about what we do not see.

Hebrews 11:1

REMAIN IN PEACE

Never let a day go by without having God in your life.

THINK POSITIVE, WORRY NOT

You are excited to be hired at your dream job and are afraid of heights. The job is on the 20th floor of a high-rise building. On your way to work, you wonder what if the elevator breaks? What if the elevator gets stuck on floor 19? What will I do?

Assure yourself that the elevator is working fine. If the elevator gets stuck, someone will rescue you. These positive thoughts get rid of fears and diminish anxiety. Your mind is at ease and you can enjoy your first day at work.

"Be careful, or your hearts will be weighed down with carousing, drunkenness and the anxieties of life, and that day will close on you suddenly like a trap.

Luke 21:34 [5]

I sought the LORD, and He answered me and delivered me from all my fears.

Psalm 34:4 [16]

THOUGHTS AND FEELINGS ARE SEPERATE

A thought is mental and can be dismissed before a feeling or physical action is involved. If you can tell the differences, the more you are in control and your anxiety levels decrease.

If you reflect on a terrible problem, it makes you sad. This is the inner thought process in action. When you are sad, you may cry. This is the action portion. When anxiety is raised, you think more about the problem which increases a response action, and in this case, it is to cry.

Another example, you are breathing fine, but in your mind, you have thoughts of having trouble with breathing. If you take this as a reality, you experience the pain of not breathing. You gasp to get air. You changed a thought concept into an action.

Tell your inner mind you know things are okay and you are breathing fine. Tell yourself God is in control. You are at peace and more relaxed. This is an effective way to calm anxiety before it escalates.

TO ESCALATE

Is to cause or become more serious or intense.

LOCATE YOUR ESCALATION LEVEL

It may seem as if anxiety is triggered from nowhere. Anxiety is an emotion sparked from a happening. You also can have anxiety thoughts about things that have not or may not even occur.

When anxiety happens, it may escalate. Pay attention to your escalation level and do not let it get past a certain point. It is easier to control it at a lower level than a higher one.

STAY WITHIN YOURSELF

See your problems through your eyes and think of what you need to do to better yourself. Do not critique yourself. It will make you unsure of yourself and actions. Get in touch with people in support of you and stay in a light uplifting mood.

TAKE CARE OF YOURSELF

At school or work, pace yourself. Your body has limitations. If you cross those limitations, anxiety increases. Take breaks when you can. You do not want to get exhausted. Work according to your own strengths. Never do what you are not equipped or defined to you.

Cast all your anxiety on Him because He cares for you. 1 Peter 5:7 1

CHAPTER 3:

STAY FOCUSED

DISCOVER WAYS TO CONTROL YOUR COMPETITIVE ANXIETY.

IN THIS CHAPTER:

v FIVE BREATHING TECHNIQUES

v FOCUS AND CENTER YOUR ATTENTION

v LET THINGS PASS

v RID NEGATIVE THOUGHTS

v WINNING FEELINGS

No position is needed to execute this exercise. You can do it sitting, laying or any other similar position. Inhale through your nose and exhale through mouth but in an even fashion.

- Take a deep breath. Allow your neck and shoulders to relax while exhaling.

- In the second breath, relax your shoulders and arms.

- In third breath, relax your stomach, and other lower parts of your body. Continue this process until every body part is relaxed.

FOCUS AND CENTER YOUR ATTENTION

To center yourself is also called focusing. You start by concentrating. Bring your thoughts to the center of your body. Focus your attention behind your navel.

This technique is done by people who play sports. Tennis, soccer and football players and others in similar games use this technique for concentration. Centering is calming and soothes the mind. It helps you focus on positive thoughts. You can execute centering with these steps:

- With your feet flat on floor and arms hanging by your sides. Stand in a loose position.

- Breathe in and out. Notice the increase and decrease of tension in your upper body when you breathe in and out.

- Inhale deep as possible. Find the tension in your chest, shoulders and abdominal areas. Exhale to get rid of any tension from your body and relieve mental stress.

- Visualize and say a calming word with every breath you take. Example words are calm, relax, serenity and loosen up. Feel free to make more words as you go along.

LET TIME ENDURE

Times may come when you let go because you cannot cope with everything you face. Let go after giving your full effort. Trust God to intervene and correct the situation.

Practice the exercises mentioned. Do not trouble yourself or become anxious. At the start, it will be difficult to calm yourself. Prayer to the LORD is the best thing you can do for yourself.

Therefore I tell you, whatever you ask for in prayer, believe that you have received it, and it will be yours. - Mark 11:24

RID NEGATIVE THOUGHTS

Make sure negative thoughts do not arise in your mind. In a somber mood, think about wanting to take part in a positive activity. Be a willing participant. It may be difficult but if you focus on a positive event you've experienced, nothing is impossible. Be sure to read your Bible regularly and choose wisely when it comes to associations and outside activities.

WINNING FEELINGS

Produce a winning mood inside yourself. Make it happen by remembering a time when you performed your best in a particular field and achieved success. It can be any life event. Bring your confidence level to a high by writing on it.

CHAPTER 4:

DISTRACTIONS

To Distract

:

Preventing someone from giving their full attention to something.

Distraction techniques are useful in diverting anxiety. You can use a distraction as an alternate to free anxious concerns. It is hard to remember things when your mind is anxious on another matter.

You may be afraid of dogs. When you see one, you stop thinking on your current happenings. Your focus is on the dog.

When your favorite meal is cooked and you are hungry, your focus is on the meal. A distraction will deter you from your current problem, so you are thinking on something else.

Provide Something Other than the Undesirable Thought

An anxious person needs a focus. The same as mentioned above, but make sure the focus is strong enough to divert a long-lasting effect. Call a friend or relative you haven't talked to in a long time. Take a nature walk or prepare yourself for a much-needed vacation.

Good thoughts and deeds lessen a phobia. You need to know a distraction is a temporary relief. When the distraction ends the anxiety may appear. In other words, a distraction may satisfy anxiety in a non-emergency situation for temporary relief.

CHAPTER 5:

MUSCLE RELAXATION TO CONTROL ANXIETY

FIND OUT HOW TO USE YOUR MUSCLES TO CONTROL ANXIETY.

- PREP FOR RELAXATION
- BREATHING
- SCAN YOUR MUSCLES FOR TENSION
- PROGRESSIVE RELAXATION

To execute muscle exercises, your body needs to be relaxed.

- You should not have any physical injuries or a history of past muscle injuries. If you do, meet with your health advisor before beginning.

- Choose an environment with low distractions. Turn off TV, radio, phones and similar devices which can distract you.

- Sit in a relaxing position in a chair, sofa or bed. Choose what is comfortable for you.

- Avoid beginning to practice these techniques if you have eaten a heavy meal or had an alcohol drink.

- Keep up with your routine with regular practice.

BREATHING

Breathing exercises are highly effective against anxiety but there are other techniques called muscle relaxation which can help in controlling anxiety long term. Follow the relaxation techniques below:

SCAN YOUR MUSCLES FOR TENSION

Consider your whole body. Try to focus on the parts where you are the most tensed after a tiring day. Make a chart of every body part including arms, legs, stomach, forehead and others. Identify the parts where there is tension. Soak in a warm tub using a light pressure and rub circular motion on those areas.

PROGRESSIVE MUSCLE RELAXATION

Progressive muscle relaxation is a technique used today. For years, people have done this effective technique. You train your muscles to respond to long-lasting anxiety.

- Familiarize yourself with the muscle groups in the body.

- Tense and release each muscle group.

- You are releasing stress and toning your body at the same time.

RELAXATION TECHNIQUES

These are good techniques to help you relax:

- Make a hand fist. Experience the tension in your forearm and hand. Hold for 5 seconds and release.

- Repeat for both arms and hands.

- Raise your eyebrows as high as you can. Notice the tension above your eyes then, release it.

- Open your mouth wide for 5 seconds. As you close your mouth the tension decreases. Contraction and release exercises are for every muscle in your body. Once you execute them, you will be energized! Execute muscle sets on different days of the week.

CHAPTER 6:

ANXIETY FROM INTERVIEWS, TEST TAKING AND MEETINGS

In this chapter, we will discuss getting rid of the test, meeting

and

interview anxieties.

v WHAT TO DO BEFORE A TEST, MEETING, OR INTERVIEW

CALM DOWN

Anxious persons have a problem staying calm when they go for an interview or take a test. The anxiety level is high, and they have a hard time controlling themselves. Techniques are available to help decrease the anxiety of an interview, test or meetings with the boss.

BEFORE THE TEST, MEETING, OR INTERVIEW

Get up half an hour earlier than usual. Make sure you are well rested from the night before. Avoid distractions by going to a quiet place in your home. Have prayer at this time. Ask God for favor, calmness, guidance and the strength to make it through with success.

Make good preparations for your meeting, test or interview. Do not overdo it. Believe the fact you have done whatever you needed to do to make your experience smooth.

Make sure you are not taking a test, interview or meeting as if your life depended upon it. Instead, be casual and stay in a light mood. More opportunities await you in the future.

For test taking, try to remember an old test you aced. Remember a meeting or interview you went on where you felt comfortable. To remember a similar event boosts your confidence. Go into an event in a positive frame of mind and observe things. Check out the environment. Be relaxed and well-prepared.

WHAT TO LOOK FOR DURING AN EVENT

When you are in middle of your event, stay calm. Do not lose your confidence. If you exert even a single wrong gesture or movement, it may ruin your entire preparation for that event. Expect that complications may arise during the event. Make sure you stay calm and in control.

Do not be anxious about anything, but in every situation, by prayer and petition, with thanksgiving, present your request to God.

                    Philippians 4:6

CONCLUSION

Our bodies are wonderfully made, in Gods image. Nothing HE makes is bad. We are individuals born with lots of emotions. Anger, anxiety and happiness are just a few. All these emotions are not bad. When any emotion is over-exerted due to extreme nervousness or a disorder, that is when trouble arises.

You've just read effective ways to control your anxiety. Also, remember controlled anxiety gives you positive energy to react in emergencies, therefore bringing you to safety. If you are anxious and rising out of control, refer to these pages. You have several hard-hitting techniques here to lower anxiety levels. Through faith and belief in God, Holy Spirit and our Savior, Jesus Christ, you have the power to overcome any obstacle.

Cast your cares on the Lord and he will sustain you; he will never let the righteous be shaken.

Psalm 55:22

GOD BLESS YOU!

OPPORTUNITY

I offer you an opportunity to accept Jesus Christ into your life as your Lord and Savior through dedication or re-dedication. Jesus is coming soon, and we want to have Him in our hearts and lives.

SAY THIS PASSAGE OUT LOUD:

Lord Jesus, I believe you are the Son of God.
You died on the cross for my sins and today, I accept you as my Lord and as my Savior. I will serve you for the rest of my life. In Jesus' name I pray. Amen

CONGRATULATIONS!

There is great joy in the Heavens!

Pray often, read the Scriptures, congregate with other worshipers, and spread the Word!

9. If you declare with your mouth, "Jesus is Lord" and believe in your heart that God raised Him from the dead you will be saved.

10. For it is with your heart that you believe and are justified, and it is with your mouth that you profess and are saved.

                      Romans 10: 9-10

8. BIBLE SCRIPTURES - NIV

1. 1 Peter 5:7

Cast all your anxiety on Him because He cares for you.

2. Philippians 4:6

Do not be anxious about anything, but in every situation, by prayer and petition, with thanksgiving, present your request to God.

3. Psalm 55:22

Cast your cares on the Lord and he will sustain you; he will never let the righteous be shaken.

4. Proverbs 12:25

Anxiety weights down the heart, but a kind word cheers it up.

5. Luke 21:34

"Be careful, or your hearts will be weighed down with carousing, drunkenness and the anxieties of life, and that day will close on you suddenly like a trap.

6. Matthew 6:25

"Therefore I tell you, do not worry about your life, what you will eat or drink, or about your body, what you will wear. Is not life more than food, and the body more than clothes?

7. Matthew 6:34

Therefore do not worry about tomorrow, for tomorrow will worry about itself. Each day has enough trouble of its own.

8. Psalm 119:170

May my supplication come before you; deliver me according to your promise.

9. Mark 10:27

Jesus looked at them and said, "With man this is impossible, but not with God; all things are possible with God".

10. Mark 11:24

Therefore I tell you, whatever you ask for in prayer, believe that you have received it, and it will be yours.

11. Hebrews 11:1

Now faith is confidence in what we hope for and assurance about what we do not see.

12. Luke 2:14

"Glory to God in the highest, and on earth peace, good will towards men!" (NT)

13. Romans 10:9-10

9. If you declare with your mouth, "Jesus is Lord" and believe in your heart that God raised Him from the dead you will be saved.

10. For it is with your heart that you believe and are justified, and it is with your mouth that you profess and are saved.

14. Psalm 27:1

The LORD is my light and my salvation; whom shall I fear? The LORD is the stronghold of my life; of whom shall I be afraid?

15. Proverbs 29:25

Fear of man will prove to be a snare, but whoever trusts in the LORD is kept safe.

16 Psalm 34:4

I sought the LORD, and He answered me and delivered me from all my fears.

1 John 4:18

There is no fear in love. But perfect love drives out fear, because fear has to do with punishment. The one who fears is not made perfect in love.

ABOUT THE AUTHOR

Glenda Coker is from Detroit, Michigan. She is a Christian, inspired writer, Foreign Language English Teacher, Licensed Therapist association and online radio motivator. She is the owner of the Blessings Store @ Teespring, which offers T-shirts and accessories. She is the author and editor of four books, which can be found on major book platforms.

Through social media, online radio shows and offline affiliations she spreads love to the world, motivating and inspiring people through the Word of God.

"If I can reach just one person, turning his or her life around by shining a positive light through the Word of God, it is a service well done. I aim for more".

Glenda Coker

Blessings Store: https://teespring.com/stores/blessings-store

Email: glendagrateful@gmail.cm

For more information, visit: https://www.linktr.ee/glendacoker

"Therefore I tell you, do not worry about your life, what you will eat or drink, or about your body, what you will wear. Is not life more than food, and the body more than clothes?

Matthew 6:25

AMEN

NOTES